3-D THRILLERS!

MONSTER TRUCKS
and Other Amazing Speed Machines

PAUL HARRISON

■SCHOLASTIC

New York • Toronto • London • Auckland
Sydney • Mexico City • New Delhi • Hong Kong

THE NEED FOR

Humans have been interested in speed ever since they discovered how to use moving transportation. You only have to look at the Roman chariot races of two thousand years ago to see how speed used to excite people. Today, automobile racing is one of the most popular ways of experiencing—and watching—speed!

▼ Formula 1

Probably the most high-profile of all motor sports is the Formula 1 Grand Prix race series. Today's cars have extremely powerful engines, are made from super-light materials, and use wide tires to get plenty of grip on the track. They are also aerodynamic, which means they are shaped so that the air doesn't slow them down as they push through it. A modern F1 car can race at speeds of over 200 miles per hour (320 kph)—that's over three times faster than a family car driving along on a freeway.

SPEED

TIRES without treads give the most GRIP, as there is more rubber touching the track. These are called "SLICKS!"

◀ NASCAR racing

NASCAR (the National Association for Stock Car Auto Racing) was founded in 1948 in Daytona Beach, Florida. Most NASCAR tracks are oval (instead of having loops and turns, as in F1). This means that drivers can maintain a constant pace and reach almost the same incredible speed as F1 drivers.

Dragsters! ▶

The fastest type of motorsport is drag racing. Dragsters sprint on short, straight courses and their huge rear tires give loads of grip. They use a fuel called nitromethane to reach speeds of up to 300 miles per hour (480 kph). They need parachutes, as well as brakes, to slow them down at the end!

WE'LL RACE

People love racing so much that they'll race almost anything—and on any surface! Farmers used to test their plowing skills by seeing how fast their horses could pull weights. This contest turned into tractor pulling!

The WEIGHT of a sled can be around 65,000 pounds (30,000 kg). That's as HEAVY as ten elephants!

▼ Pull that load!

In the first tractor pulling competitions, people would jump onto a sled pulled by a tractor to make it heavier. This was very dangerous because the tractor would be moving at the time. As tractors became more powerful, they pulled weights instead of people.

HNYTHING...

How sleds work ▶

Sleds are trailers with heavy weights attached.
The idea of a tractor-pulling competition is
to see how far a tractor or truck can drag
a sled along a straight, 300-foot
(90-m) course. The tractor to go
the farthest is the winner. The
weights are designed to get
heavier the farther the tractor
travels, which makes pulling
more and more difficult.

▼ Mud bogging!

Mud racing, or mud bogging, is just
like it sounds—a wheel-spinning sprint
down a muddy track. The trucks race two at
a time to the finish line—if they get that far!

MEETING THE

With massive wheels and decorated cabs, monster trucks look like nothing else on the road! But why were they invented and what can they do? In the 1970s drivers were modifying their pickup trucks and, as the sports of tractor pulling and mud bogging became popular, one thing led to another ...

▼ In the beginning

The birth of the monster truck started with a guy named Bob Chandler. In the mid-1970s he began to change his Ford pickup truck so that it would run better when he drove it off-road. He added extra-large tires and kept making the vehicle bigger and better. Before long, Bob and his truck, nicknamed Bigfoot, became well known. They were soon a star attraction, appearing at truck pulling and other automobile events.

MUNSTERS

▲ Big three

In the early days of monster trucks, drivers were often loyal to a particular brand of vehicle. The favorite manufacturers were Ford, Dodge, and Chevrolet. As truck sports grew more popular, these three companies started to sponsor drivers.

▼ Bigger is better

One way to make a big impression is to have the biggest wheels around! But monster wheels can't be squeezed in under normal wheel arches, so the suspension (the bar that stops the ride from being too bumpy) has to be raised up so the wheels fit underneath. It's a huge climb to reach the cab!

CRUNCH!

For fans of monster trucks, looks aren't the only important thing. Fans also love them for their wrecking ability—stomping on and jumping over other cars. Car crushing and distance jumping are exciting to watch and really pull in the crowds!

▼ Car crushing ...

As tires grew bigger and the suspension was lifted up higher, people began to wonder what the trucks could do, apart from go off-road. In 1981, Bob Chandler and Bigfoot did something that monster trucks are now renowned for—they crushed cars! Bob drove Bigfoot over two wrecked cars in a farmer's field and filmed the stunt just for fun. Soon after, Bob was asked to repeat the feat at a truck-pulling event ... and history was made!

▼ ... and big jumping!

It wasn't long before monster trucks were doing all sorts of tricks and stunts, such as jumping off ramps. Wheelies (lifting the front wheels off the ground) and donuts (spinning the truck round and round) also became part of the show. As monster truck racing began to increase in popularity in the 1980s, freestyle events were held. These gave drivers the chance to show the crazy things they could do!

▲ Black Stallion

Soon people were competing to see who could jump the farthest. Dan Runte, in Bigfoot 14, jumped over a Boeing 727 airplane, making a world record leap of 202 feet (61.5 m). Another notable record was made by the truck Black Stallion, which jumped 70 feet (21 m)—backwards!

UNDER THE

Monster trucks
have come a long
way from their
start as ordinary
pickup trucks. Now
they are expensive
hi-tech machines,
ready to face
anything!

Body parts ▶

Truck bodies are made from one big
piece of fiberglass. This material can
be molded into whacky shapes. Best
of all, it can easily be removed and
replaced if it gets damaged—which
happens a lot! The doors don't open,
so the driver climbs in through
a trapdoor in the roof.

Bounce
the bumps ▶

The part of the truck that stops
the ride from being too bumpy is called
the suspension. When you bounce over
cars or land from a jump, you want the
impact to be as soft as possible. Monster
trucks don't have springs like ordinary
cars, but gas-filled tubes that are good
for absorbing the bumps.

SKIN

It's not only the FRONT wheels that steer on a monster truck. The REAR wheels also steer, so you can turn in tight places!

▼ What a whopper!

A monster truck weighs around 10,000 pounds (4,500 kg) and travels at around 80 miles per hour (130 kph), so it needs a big engine to do the job. The engine doesn't use normal gas or diesel, but a special alcohol and fuel mix for added performance. In one run, a truck can burn 2.5 gallons (9.5 l) of fuel. In most trucks, the engine is mounted just behind the driver, who wears a protective suit in case of fire. The driver also wears safety belts and a helmet. Inside the cab are strong bars, like a cage, for protection if the truck rolls over.

IT's A STAR

When monster trucks started to compete against one another, they began to draw their own fans. Many of the monster trucks became stars and attracted a dedicated following. Here are a few of the really famous ones.

▼ More Bigfoots

Bigfoot was the original monster truck. As the audiences for monster truck shows grew, Bob Chandler and his team made more vehicles to keep up with demand. There have been over 17 different models, but the world's biggest monster race truck is Bigfoot 5 (below). It's a whopping 15 feet, 6 inches (4.7 m) high! The tires alone are 10 feet (3.04 m) high.

Firestone

BIGFOOT

48X68

ON WHEELS!

Samson ▶

The fiberglass bodies of the trucks can be molded into any shape. Here this technique has been used cleverly on a truck called Samson, named after the superstrong man in the Bible.

▼ Grave Digger

When Dennis Anderson wanted to build a mud-bogging truck, he stopped where his budget allowed--at the junkyard! When other competitors saw his creation, they laughed at him, but he famously replied, "I'll take this old junk and dig your grave!" Soon after, Grave Digger was born. The original was a battered old pickup from the 1950s, but today there are many different Grave Diggers. The vehicle shown here is Grave Digger #19.

EVEN MORE

Trucks aren't the only machines to have been given the monster treatment. Really big vehicles are often used in farming and industry as well. Here are a few of those monsters—and a mini-monster, too!

▼ Monster tractors

As farms became larger and more mechanized, farmers needed bigger machinery to work in the fields— so tractors grew! The title for the world's biggest tractor goes to a machine known as Big Roy. Originally built in the 1970s, this tractor is now on display at Manitoba Agricultural Museum. Big Roy is 30 feet (9.1 m) long, has eight-wheel drive, air suspension, and, of course, an enormous engine!

MONSTERS

Mini-monster trucks ▶

Radio-controlled monster trucks are almost as much fun as the real thing! These mini-beasts travel at up to 45 miles per hour (70 kph)—as well as performing the usual jumps and stunts! People race them at monster truck events.

▼ Earth movers

The biggest trucks, like the one below, are built for the mining industry. The bigger the truck, the more dirt and rubble it can move. The cab is so far off the ground that the driver needs stairs to climb in!

PUTTIN' ON A

A monster truck show is also called a jamboree. No other sport combines jumps, crashes, dirt, and fire in quite the same way! Here are some of the crazy events you'll find there ...

▲ Let's freestyle!

In addition to racing, jumping, and car crushing, there may be freestyle stunt competitions at a jamboree, such as the tire burnout. This is when the back wheels spin like crazy, but the truck doesn't move.

Robosaurus ▶

This oversized, robotic dinosaur is a popular act at jamborees. Built for entertainment, it breathes fire and chews up cars for breakfast! It took two years and cost over $2 million to build.

SHOW

MONSTER TRUCKS are not thought to be safe enough to use on the road. They have to be transported in trucks to each JAMBOREE!

▼ Fun at the fair

Jamborees are fun for motorsport fans. On top of all the monster truck action, there are warm-up acts, such as motocross, where off-road motorcycles race around the track. Or there may be motorcycle stunt riding or a demolition derby, where cars race around and smash into one another. It's also a great place for fans to buy and sell everything, from spare parts to souvenirs and from T-shirts to hot dogs!

SPEED ON TWO

Many motorsport fans are into the art of racing on two wheels rather than four. The speed of these machines depends on their light weight—a little power goes a long way!

▼ MotoGP

The motorcycle version of Formula 1 is known as MotoGP. MotoGP bikes are built purely for racing, and they all have the same-sized engines to make the competition even. This means that the skill of the rider counts for everything. The sport is very dangerous. There is nothing between the rider and the road, so a small mistake can mean a nasty crash. MotoGP racing takes place all over the world, but one place to watch it in the United States is at the Indianapolis Motor Speedway.

WHEELS

▲ Drag bikes

Like dragster cars, there are also drag bikes. The bikes are super-streamlined for a smooth shape, which helps to travel through the air quickly. The rider lies forward in the saddle for the same reason. Drag bikes can travel up to 170 miles per hour (275 kph) over a short track.

▼ World record breaker!

The fastest thing on two wheels is the Top 1 Oil "Ack Attack" Streamliner. This amazing vehicle broke the world two-wheeled land speed record in 2010. It reached a staggering 376.363 miles per hour (605.698 kph) at the Bonneville Salt Flats in Utah.

FASTEST ON

G oing fast isn't enough for some people. They want to go the fastest! Since the days of the first automobiles, speed has been an important part of driving. Here are some of the fastest cars on Earth!

◀ It's a Bluebird

The first land speed record was set in 1898 by a Frenchman traveling in a battery-powered car at 39 miles per hour (63 kph). Then, in 1924, Malcolm Campbell set the first of his nine land speed records. The last seven of these were set in cars that he named Bluebird. In 1964, his son Donald set the record in a jet-powered Bluebird, at 403.1 miles per hour (648.7 kph).

LAND!

▼ The Turbinator!

There are different categories of land speed record because there are different ways of powering a car. In an ordinary car, the engine drives the wheels. But in a jet-powered car, the vehicle is fitted with a turbine, a machine that uses burning gases to blast the car along. The record for a wheel-driven car stands at 458.1 miles per hour (737.3 kph), set by a vehicle called Turbinator at Bonneville Salt Flats, Utah, in 2001.

▲ Thrusting speed

The holder of the absolute world land speed record is Thrust SSC. Thrust is basically a jet engine with a seat and wheels attached! In 1997, it recorded an incredible 763 miles per hour (1227.9 kph). SSC stands for "supersonic car." Supersonic means faster than the speed of sound. Thrust SSC is the only car to have achieved that feat.

ON THE RAILS

B efore the 1800s, the only way to travel faster than running speed was on horseback. Then, during the age of steam, the locomotive arrived. The world changed and ordinary people could now travel much faster (and farther!) than ever before.

▲ Steaming ahead

Steam locomotives developed steadily during the 19th and early 20th centuries. In 1934, in the United Kingdom, the Flying Scotsman became the first train to travel at 100 miles per hour (160 kph). The record for the fastest steam locomotive ever belongs to Mallard, pictured above, which reached 126 miles per hour (202 kph) four years later. This remains the official record for steam locomotives.

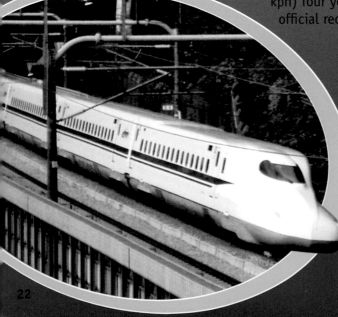

◄ Like a bullet!

The bullet train, named after the shape of the train's nose, has been running in Japan since 1964. Also known as the *shinkansen*, a new version of this train was launched in 2011. It has a top speed of 186 miles per hour (300 kph).

▼ And even faster ...

Believe it or not, there are other trains in everyday use that are even faster than the bullet train. One is the French TGV (*train à grande vitesse* or "high speed train"). Its normal running speed is around 200 miles per hour (320 kph), but under test conditions the TGV managed to break 310 miles per hour (500 kph)! Like the bullet train, the TGV is powered by electricity from cables that run above the train. However, the fastest passenger locomotive in the world today runs in China. Launched in December 2010, the CRH380A, shown below, is designed to run at 236 miles per hour (380 kph)!

In the United States, the FASTEST train currently runs at 150 miles per hour (241 kph) between Boston and Washington, DC.

WUNDERS UN

For most people, traveling on water means taking a ride in a row boat or on a ferry. But some daredevils need to get their thrills with a bit of high-speed water action!

▼ Bumpy ride

The problem with water is that it slows boats down, as they have to push through it to move. Boats that skim across the top of the water can go much faster. That's why offshore powerboat racing is the fastest type of boat racing around. Some powerboats are capable of traveling at around 170 miles per hour (273 kph)— nearly as fast as an F1 racecar.

WATER

Spirit of Australia ▶

In 1978, Ken Warby set a water speed record of 319.627 miles per hour (514.39 kph) in a boat called the *Spirit of Australia*. Powered by a jet engine, it has yet to be beaten and is now on display at the National Maritime Museum in Sydney, Australia.

Bluebird K7 ▼

Perhaps the most famous water speed record breaker is *Bluebird K7*, piloted by Donald Campbell, who also broke the land speed record. Between 1955 and 1964, he broke the water speed record seven times.

FAST FLIERS!

The history of powered air travel is amazingly short. The first flight was made in 1903. In just over a 100 years, airplanes have developed from flimsy machines made from string and wood into space probes that can fly outside Earth's atmosphere. They can even reach other planets.

▲ It's a bird!

When a car travels along a road, a force called friction acts between the road and the car tires. This slows the car down. Air creates less friction than the ground or water, which is why airborne vehicles are the quickest speed machines around. The fastest jet plane is the SR-71 Blackbird spy plane, which travels at Mach 3.2—that's 3.2 times the speed of sound!

To boldly go ... ▶

The fastest vehicles ever created are space probes. For instance, *Galileo*, shown here, is believed to be one of the fastest. In 1995, it entered Jupiter's atmosphere at an incredible 108,000 miles per hour (173,809 kph).

When a plane breaks the SPEED OF SOUND, this makes a loud noise, like a thunder clap, called a SONIC BOOM!

▼ Concorde

The fastest passenger airplane ever in service was the Concorde, a joint venture between the United Kingdom and France. It traveled at speeds up to Mach 2.2, completing the journey between New York and London in just 3.5 hours. The Concorde is no longer in operation and supersonic flight, which is faster than the speed of sound, is now confined to military aircraft and spacecraft.

THE FUTURE

A look at the speed records in this book shows that it has been a while since many of them were broken. Does this mean we have now reached our speed limit? Or might machines of the future go even faster? Well, it looks like new speed machines could be on their way.

▼ Friction free

One challenge to traveling quickly is friction. The theory is that if you decrease friction, you can increase speed. This is the idea behind trains known as maglevs, which stands for "magnetic levitation." As the name suggests, maglevs use magnets to hover above a rail line, while an electrical charge pushes the train along. Maglevs are in use in China, and are being tested in Japan and Germany. The anticipated top speed of 550 miles per hour (885 kph) is pretty fast!

OF SPEED

▲ Scram!

The Boeing X-51 Scramjet is an unmanned aircraft for testing hypersonic flying. Hypersonic means very high supersonic speeds of Mach 5 and above—five times the speed of sound! X-51 undertook its first free flight in 2010 and was able to sustain a flight at over Mach 5.

▼ Power to the people

Some scientists predict that we will run out of oil and coal in as few as 50 years, so we need to think about new sources of energy. Therefore, the future may lie in electric cars powered by battery or solar (Sun) power. At the moment, solar powered cars don't go very fast—but who knows? Perhaps they will become the speed machines of the future!

MONSTER

N ow that you've raced through the world of monster trucks, top-speed vehicles, and record breakers, perhaps you think you've seen it all? Well, here are a few more fast facts to turn you into a total speed freak!

The WORLD'S biggest land vehicle is a digger used for mining. It is 311 feet (94 m) tall and is as HEAVY as an ocean liner!

▼ Formula ... Rossa!

The fastest rollercoaster on the planet is called Formula Rossa and it runs at Ferrari World in Abu Dhabi. Shaped like a Ferrari race car, it accelerates up to a speed of 149 miles per hour (240 kph), so riders can feel what it's like to drive a real Formula 1 car!

FACTS

▼ Maximum Overkill

The world's fastest monster truck is called Maximum Overkill. Driver Kirk Dabney set a new speed record in 2009 at 90.44 miles per hour (145.54 kph)!

◀ Girl power

Monster trucks can be a girl thing, too! One of the best-known female drivers is Madusa. A professional wrestler, she started monster truck driving in 2003 and now holds several championship titles.

This edition created in 2012 by
Arcturus Publishing Limited, 26/27 Bickels Yard,
151–153 Bermondsey Street, London SE1 3HA

ISBN 978-0-545-43422-5

10 9 8 7 6 5 4 3 2 1   12 13 14 15 16

Printed in Malaysia 106

First Scholastic edition, August 2012

ARCTURUS CREDITS
Author: Paul Harrison
Editors: Lisa Miles and Kate Overy
Designer: Tania Rösler
Illustrator (glasses): Ian Thompson

PICTURE CREDITS
Alamy: p. 31 bottom
Alvey and Towers: p. 4 bottom, p. 5 top
Andrew Fielder: front cover, p. 1 center, p. 6
bottom, p. 7 top and bottom
Corbis: p. 2 bottom, p. 3 top, p. 17 bottom,
p. 19 top, p. 22 top, p. 24 bottom, p. 27 bottom
Empics: p. 25 bottom
Getty: p. 20 bottom, p. 21 bottom
Liebherr: p. 15 bottom
Monster Photos: p. 8 bottom, p. 9 top and
bottom, p.10 top, p.11 bottom, p. 13 top
Mxnewsfeed.com: p. 19 bottom
Paolo Keller: p. 30 bottom

Paul de Joode: p. 15 top
Rcmotorsports.com: p. 31 top
Rex Features: p. 12 bottom, p. 23 bottom,
p. 25 top
Shutterstock: p. 3 bottom, p. 5 bottom,
p.10 bottom, p. 13 bottom, p. 16 top and
bottom, p. 28 bottom, back cover
Science Photo Library: p.20–21 top, p. 26
bottom, p. 26–27 top, p.29 bottom
Wikimedia: p. 14 bottom, p. 22 bottom,
p. 29 top

3-D images produced by Pinsharp 3-D Graphics